MY LITTLE GOLDEN BOOK ABOUT
K-POP

By Jessica Yoon • Illustrated by Suji Park

For Melissa, Larry, Debbi, and Talia (again) —J.Y.
For mom, my forever star —S.P.

Golden Books
An imprint of Random House Children's Books
A division of Penguin Random House LLC
1745 Broadway, New York, NY 10019
penguinrandomhouse.com
rhcbooks.com

Library of Congress Cataloging-in-Publication Data is available upon request.
ISBN 979-8-217-23314-4 (trade) — ISBN 979-8-217-23321-2 (ebook)
Manufactured in the United States of America
10 9 8 7 6 5 4 3 2 1
EU Contact: Penguin Random House Ireland, 32 Nassau Street, Dublin D02 YH68.
https://eu-contact.penguin.ie

Girls' Generation
BTS
BLACKPINK

K-pop is short for Korean popular music, a blend of pop, hip-hop, R&B, electronic music, and more! K-pop also features high-energy choreography and eye-catching visuals.

Modern K-pop began in the 1990s. Over time, its popularity spread to other countries in a phenomenon called Hallyu, or "the Korean wave." Today, there are millions of K-pop fans all over the world!

Seo Taiji and Boys are considered the first modern K-pop group. In 1992, they debuted the song "난 알아요 (I Know)" on a live televised talent show. Their performance included rap, rock, and breakdancing. The group received the lowest score of the night. But teen viewers loved them! Their song topped the music charts for weeks.

Seo Taiji and Boys paved the way for the first wave of K-pop. This included groups like H.O.T., Sechs Kies, S.E.S., Fin.K.L, g.o.d, and Shinhwa.

In 1996, H.O.T. released their iconic song "Candy." The ski clothes they wore in the music video led to a fashion craze. Everyone wanted fluffy mittens!

S.E.S.

Shoo Bada (Sea) Eugene

Hyunjin (Stray Kids)

S.E.S. was one of the first K-pop girl groups. Right before a new tour, they dyed their hair different colors. This change got them banned from South Korean TV shows. But it didn't stop fans from buying their albums! Now K-pop idols express themselves with all different hair colors.

Yeji (ITZY)

j-hope (BTS)

Taeyong (NCT) Soobin (TXT) Dahyun (TWICE)

When South Korea faced hard times, the government realized K-pop's popularity could help the country. They supported entertainment companies that created the idol training system to find more K-pop stars. Trainees practiced singing and dancing, worked hard, and followed strict rules—all in the hopes of becoming famous. These training programs still exist today.

By the 2000s, second-generation K-pop groups, like TVXQ, Girls' Generation, BIGBANG, Wonder Girls, 2NE1, and SHINee, became famous throughout Asia. Solo artists like Rain and BoA—the Queen of K-pop—gained popularity, too. They began to release songs in different languages to reach more fans.

TVXQ and Girls' Generation were the first to include photo cards in their albums. Fans collected and traded these cards—something they still do today!

TVXQ was also the first group to create an official fandom name—Cassiopeia. Now all K-pop fandoms have their own names!

BIGBANG, known as the Kings of K-pop, started a new fad, too. In 2006, they introduced crown-shaped light sticks designed by G-Dragon, one of the group's members. Now custom light sticks are a huge part of every K-pop concert experience. Fans love waving their light sticks in unison to create a light show!

G-Dragon also started a trend where celebrities treat airports like fashion runways. He and other K-pop idols, like Hwasa from MAMAMOO and Hanni from NewJeans, use their travel outfits to give fans style inspiration!

In 2012, K-pop became even more popular with PSY's hit song "Gangnam Style." PSY's catchy song and dance moves became a pop culture phenomenon. The music video, which also features the K-pop star Hyuna, became the first YouTube video ever to reach one billion views!

In the 2010s, YouTube and social media helped propel the third generation of K-pop idols to global stardom. This included groups like BTS, BLACKPINK, EXO, TWICE, SEVENTEEN, and Red Velvet.

Third-generation groups focused on telling stories with their songs to connect with fans. They also made high-quality music videos that looked like scenes from movies!

Fan-favorite group BTS has won hundreds of awards and set many world records for song streams, video views, and album sales!

Its members sing about self-love, mental health, and following your dreams. They also promote these ideas off-stage, by working for social causes and sharing their positive messages with world leaders. Their fans, called ARMY, love their dynamite mix of singing, rapping, and dance moves.

During this time, entertainment companies looked for talent in other countries, too. For example, while BLACKPINK's members Jisoo and Jennie auditioned in Seoul, South Korea, Rosé was recruited from Australia and Lisa was recruited from Thailand.

Today, they light up the sky together as one of the world's most popular girl groups. Their fans—BLINKs—love their hit songs about being strong and confident girls. BLACKPINK was the first Asian headliner at the Coachella music festival in California!

The fourth generation of K-pop started in 2018. It included groups like Stray Kids, aespa, ITZY, TOMORROW X TOGETHER, and ENHYPEN. Idols from this generation were especially good at using social media. They would sometimes gain international fans before they even debuted!

The group Stray Kids was formed on a Korean reality show. They have broken several records with their chart-topping albums!

Manon Yoonchae

Daniela Lara

Sophia

Megan

The year 2023 marked the start of fifth-generation groups. This includes ZEROBASEONE, RIIZE, BOYNEXTDOOR, BABYMONSTER, and KATSEYE. Some of these groups were formed on reality competitions.

KATSEYE's show aired on YouTube. With members from three continents, they are considered the first global girl group!

The group BABYMONSTER was supposed to debut with only five members. But fans loved all seven trainees so much, the entertainment company decided to debut them all!

HUNTR/X

Mira

Zoey

Rumi

K-pop is so popular that even animated idols can break records! In 2025, Sony Entertainment released the film *KPop Demon Hunters*. The movie included characters from Korean folklore, like the beloved tiger and magpie, and of course everything K-pop!

The movie's K-pop groups, HUNTR/X and Saja Boys, both hit the *Billboard* charts with songs like "Golden" and "Soda Pop." Three TWICE members—Jeongyeon, Jihyo, and Chaeyoung—recorded a version of the song "Takedown" just for the movie!

The award-winning film became Netflix's most-viewed movie ever, creating a whole new generation of K-pop fans!

The popularity of K-pop shows how music has the power to bring people together across languages and cultures. It is also a way to learn about Korean people and their history, and to make the world a more inclusive place. In the future, K-pop will continue to push boundaries, always evolving for the fans!